Pets with Tourette's

**Mike Lepine &
Mark Leigh**

 **Skyhorse Publishing**

Skyhorse Publishing books may be purchased in bulk at special discounts for sales promotion, corporate gifts, fund raising, or educational purposes. Special editions can also be created to specifications. For details, contact Special Sales Department, Skyhorse Publishing, 555 Eighth Avenue, Suite 903, New York, NY 10018 or info@skyhorsepublishing.com.

www.skyhorsepublishing.com

10 9 8 7 6 5 4 3 2 1

ISBN 10: 1-60239-365-6
ISBN 13: 978-1-60239-365-3

Printed in China

For Zippy, the rudest cat in the history of cats

Thank-yous

The authors would like to thank the following people for their assistance and tolerance: Philippa Hatton-Lepine, Gage Hatton-Lepine, Rob Shreeve, Debbie Leigh, Polly and Barney Leigh (kids—don't ever read this book), and Robert Day—who wanted to be mentioned in a tasteful and sophisticated work of literature.

Meet the authors

Mike Lepine and Mark Leigh have had over thirty humor and trivia books published, including three number-one bestsellers. Celebrities they have worked with include Adrian Edmondson, Julian Clary, Des Lynam, Jeremy Beadle, Roy Chubby Brown, Chris Tarrant, and Rolf Harris.

They have also written and developed numerous TV programs and recently completed their first comedy film screenplay (it's really funny and they are eagerly awaiting a top Hollywood movie agent or studio exec to contact them).

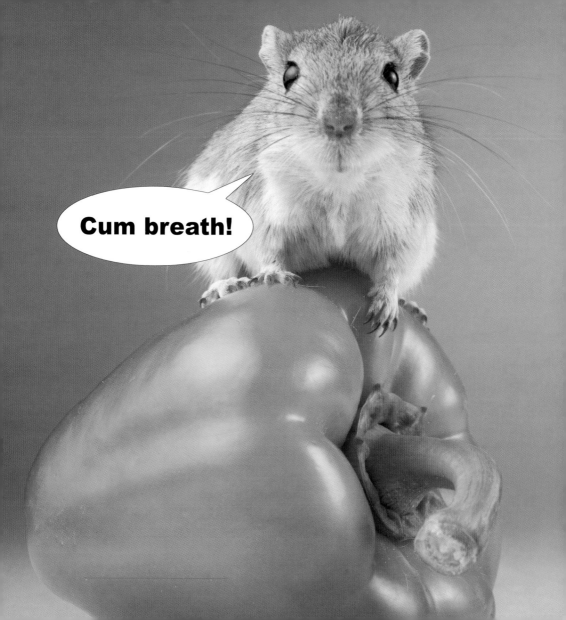